CONTENTS

You might think the whole world has been explored but large parts are still unknown territory. In the depths of the sea live hundreds of thousands of creatures we haven't yet encountered.

NORTH AMERICA

The Gulf Stream is a warm, powerful and fast current that flows from the Gulf of Mexico to the Arctic O...

SOUTH AMERICA

Pacific Ocean

Thousands of undercurrents keep the seas in motion. Together, they form five great circles, the ocean currents.

RIVERS

All over the earth we find rivers, large and small, whose tributaries reach to the far corners of the planet. Whether meandering or carving powerfully through the landscape, rivers determine our way of being in the world. They present pathways for explorers and obstacles for armies. We rely on them as sources of drinking water, for fishing and for irrigating our fields. By gravity, rivers empty into oceans, lakes, swamps or other rivers. We harness the power of flowing water to drive machines that generate power. Understanding rivers helps us to understand history and the people who have lived alongside them for centuries.

Arctic Ocean

Arctic Circle

Low tide

High tide

High tide

Low tide

Twice a day the oceans' waters rise and fall. These tides are caused by the moon's gravitational pull and influenced by the sun. A spring tide occurs when the earth, moon and sun are lined up. During spring tides, the high tides are very high and the low tides extra low. When the sun and the moon form a right angle with the earth, there is the least difference between high and low tides, called neap tides.

EUROPE

ASIA

Pacific Ocean

Tropic of Cancer

AFRICA

Equator

Indian Ocean

Atlantic Ocean

Tropic of Capricorn

The 5 oceans

OCEANIA

Oceans are larger and deeper than seas. A sea is a mass of water on a continental shelf. Where the continent ends, the ocean begins.

There are five oceans, all connected and forming a huge mass of salt water that covers 71% of the earth's surface.

Southern Ocean

Antarctic Circle

The blue whale is the largest animal ever to have lived on Earth. It can grow to 27 m (89 ft) long and its tongue can weigh as much as an elephant.

Northern Europeans have fished herring for centuries. A school of herring might contain 10 million fish.

The mythical hunter Finn MacCool burnt himself while cooking the Salmon of Knowledge. Sucking his finger to ease the pain, he gained all the world's knowledge.

Iceland

Norwegian Sea

North Sea

Norway

Sweden

Skagerrak

Kattegat

Denmark

Ireland

Irish Sea

United Kingdom

Thames

Celtic Sea

English Channel

Netherlands

Scheldt

Belgium

Meuse

Elbe

Rhine

Germany

Czech Republic

Seine

Loire

Austria

France

Switzerland

Po

Slovenia

Cro...

Atlantic Ocean

Bay of Biscay

Ligurian Sea

Adriatic Sea

Corsica

Tiber

Italy

Spain

Portugal

Tagus

Mediterranean Sea

Sardinia

Tyrrhenian Sea

Strait of Gibraltar

Sicily

The kingfisher is a piscivore: it eats fish, so likes to live near running water.

A large marker stone lies at the Thames' source in the Cotswold Hills.

Ancient Britons believed that gods lived in the river. Old Father Thames was the Thames' river god.

The city of Oxford is known for its university, which is nearly 1000 years old.

Archaeologists have found objects in the Thames from the Neolithic Ag...

Rare black swans live in Marlow.

The river once had two names: some called it the Isis, others the Thames.

The rich role of the Thames in Britain's past inspired politician John Burns to describe the river as "liquid history."

The name Thames comes from the Celtic *tamesas*, meaning *dark*.

The Boat Race at Henley is a rowin... contest between the universities of Oxfo... and Cambridge, first held in 1829.

Cherwell

Thames

UNITED KINGDOM

6

The Thames is the idyllic setting for *The Wind in the Willows*, a children's book by Kenneth Grahame, published in 1908.

From its source in the Cotswold Hills, the **Thames** wends its way down to join the Cherwell at Oxford. The river flows past Henley, the royal residence of Windsor Castle, Eton College and through London to the North Sea. From Teddington Lock the Thames becomes tidal—this stretch is called Tideway. In London the water level can rise up to 7 m (23 ft) during spring tides.

The Romans invaded Britain in 43 CE. They built their headquarters, Londinium, on the north bank of the Thames.

The Port of London has been important since Roman times. Ships could moor in the middle of the city and ply their trade. Over centuries the port moved closer to the river's mouth with goods transported to the interior by road or rail.

The avocet was thought to be extinct in England by 1840 but since 1947 has been sighted in the wild.

London Bridge

Foulness Island

Two Tree Island

Isle of Sheppey

In Greenwich lies the prime meridian—the zero point used for measuring longitude. Standard time, or Greenwich Mean Time (GMT), is also determined from here.

The Thames Tunnel under the river was dug between 1825 and 1843. Originally built for horse-drawn carriages, it is now part of London's transport network.

The Thames Barrier is a dam that protects London against exceptional high tides. The gates rest on the bottom of the river and can be raised when necessary.

Frost fairs were held annually on the frozen Thames during the Little Ice Age, between the 17th and 19th centuries.

North Sea

An estuary is a wide river mouth where salt and fresh water mingle to form brackish water.

Elbe

GERMANY

Martin Luther nailed his 95 theses to the door of the Wittenberg church in the early 16th century to protest against practices in the Catholic Church. This led to the Reformation and a new movement in Christianity: Protestantism.

The Elbe was the eastern border of the empire of Charlemagne (768–814).

The white-tailed sea eagle is the biggest bird of prey in Europe.

Canal bridge, Magdeburg

The Magdeburg hemispheres were used to demonstrate the strength of air pressure in 1654. The copper hemispheres were held together and sealed by a vacuum. During the demonstration 16 horses could not pull the hemispheres apart because the pressure of the outside air was too strong.

Saale

Beavers live near water. They build dams and canals to regulate the water levels in their lodges.

Elbe beaver

The Great Eagle was a 16th-century warship in service to the city of Lübeck. It was the biggest ship of its day, built to protect the trade of the Hanseatic League—a trading alliance of northern cities.

The **Elbe** begins in the Giant Mountains in the Czech Republic, near the border with Poland. From there it flows through the Ore Mountains near Saxony and over the North German Plain. It empties into the North Sea near Hamburg, via a fan-shaped estuary. One-third of the Elbe passes through the Czech Republic and two-thirds through Germany. The Elbe formed an important natural European border, marking Charlemagne's eastern boundary during his rule in the early Middle Ages; after World War II it formed part of the demarcation between East and West Germany.

Travel

Berlin

During World War II,
Nazis were fighting the US forces
in the west and the Soviet
troops... In April 1945, US and Soviet
forces met at the Elbe river, splitting
the German army.

POLAND

Dresden is still rebuilding its pre-war
Baroque character following its complete
destruction by Allied bombing in 1945.

According to a Jewish story, Rabbi Löw
of Prague made a golem—a figure
kneaded from clay of the Vltava
riverbank that came to life.

Pančava waterfall

The legendary giant Rübezahl ruled in
the Giant Mountains, source of the Elbe.

CZECH REPUBLIC

9

SWEDEN

FINLAND

Baltic Sea

ESTONIA

Neva

Saint Petersburg is an important port, the cultural capital of Russia and its second-largest city. It has 80 theatres, 62 cinemas, 2000 libraries and more than 200 museums.

LATVIA

Russia

LITHUANIA

In antiquity, the Dnieper River formed part of the Amber Road trading route. Amber is the fossilized resin from coniferous trees, sometimes called the gold of the north.

POLAND

BELARUS

A nuclear power station in Chernobyl exploded in 1986, releasing dangerous radioactive material.

Dnieper

Half of Russia's biggest cities, including its capital Moscow, are in the Dnieper's catchment.

UKRAINE

Pripyat

The Varangians were a Viking group who ruled Kievan Rus in the late 9th century, growing it into a prosperous kingdom. Kiev is now the capital of Ukraine and one of the largest cities in Eastern Europe.

The Motherland Calls is an 85 m (280 ft) memorial to World War II's Battle of Stalingrad. It stands in Volgograd, formerly Stalingrad.

MOLDOVA

Smews breed in the vast forests of Russia's north but migrate south towards the Black Sea during the winter.

ROMANIA

The mutiny on the Potemkin in 1905 is regarded as one of the important preludes to the Russian Revolution. The ship's crew refused to eat rotten meat and revolted against their officers. They took over the ship and returned to the port city of Odessa, where more ships joined the rebellion.

Ancient Greek historian Herodotus pronounced the Dnieper (then called Borysthenes) the most valuable and productive river after the Nile for its clear drinking water and abundant fish.

Black Sea

The Black Sea was named Inhospitable Sea in ancient Greek myths and subsequent names have reflected its stormy nature.

The Russian desman is a kind of mole that lives in a riverbank hole whose entrance is hidden under water. It hunts at night, digging away at the bottom of the river in search of small prey.

The **Volga** is Europe's longest river and the most important in Russia. It was called Mother Volga by the Russian people, half of whom live in its catchment. (A river's catchment or basin is the area from which water drains towards the river.) The Volga begins in the Valdai Hills and empties into the Caspian Sea. Its river basin comprises some 151,000 rivers and streams.

The **Dnieper** also begins in the Valdai Hills and travels in a southerly direction via Russia, Belarus and Ukraine to the Black Sea. The Dnieper has been an important transportation link between the Baltic Sea and the Black Sea.

A vodyanoy is a water sprite from Slavic folklore. It enslaves drowned people, taking them to its underwater palace made of sunken ships.

RUSSIA

Kama

The Volga and the Kama are now linked by reservoirs and hydroelectric plants, following a massive construction programme launched in the 1930s by the former Soviet Union.

The Huns were a nomadic group of horse riders who came to Europe from the East. They reached the Volga around 370 CE. From the 5th century the Huns raided a great deal of Europe.

Volga

...h is known for its caviar—made from the eggs of the sturgeon.

KAZAKHSTAN

Southern Buh

During the Battle of Stalingrad, the Soviet Red Army defeated Nazi Germany's army on the banks of the Volga. It was probably the bloodiest battle ever, with 1.9 million people slaughtered over six months.

The Caspian Sea is the world's largest enclosed body of water.

Caspian Sea

Around 3000 Eurasian lynx live in Scandinavia.

The northern lights (aurora borealis) are a nighttime dance of light. The northern and southern lights (aurora australis) are caused by charged solar particles attracted by Earth's magnetic poles. According to Norse mythology, the lights are reflections from the shields and weapons of the valkyries, goddesses of war.

The discovery of petroleum and natural gas in the Norwegian Sea in the 1970s brought prosperity to Norway.

Norwegian Sea

Fjords are long, narrow fingers of sea reaching inland that developed from water erosion during the Ice Age. Some are astonishingly deep, reaching well below sea level.

The Atlantic or European salmon leaves the sea and swims upriver to spawn.

In the 9th century Scandinavian Norsemen began to plunder the shores of Europe. They colonized large parts of Europe during the Viking Age (ca. 740–1050).

Sweden is approximately 60% forest and 10% water and has about 95,700 lakes.

A Norse saying: There's no such thing as bad weather, only the wrong clothes.

NORWAY

Oslo, Norway's capital city, has 40 islands, 343 lakes and a forest within its city boundaries.

The Swedish capital, Stockholm, is built on 14 islands, linked by 57 bridges.

North Sea

SWEDEN

The Little Mermaid is a famous statue in the Danish capital of Copenhagen based on a fairytale by H. C. Andersen.

Denmark

Kattegat

Baltic Sea

The Greenland shark can live up to 400 years—longer than any other vertebrate.

Barents Sea

The Alyosha Monument in the port of Murmansk remembers soldiers who defended the Soviet Arctic in World War II.

The trolls of folklore live in remote mountains and forests. These uncongenial giants eat human flesh and can't stand the sound of church bells.

Torne

FINLAND

Finland, "land of a thousand lakes," actually has about 188,000 lakes.

Gulf of Bothnia

White Sea

Bäckahästen is a mythological river-horse that drowns its riders.

Some streets in Helsinki, Finland's capital, have underground heating.

RUSSIA

Lake Onega

Lake Ladoga

Some rivers are used as roads when they freeze solid, such as the Tana in Norway, the Lena in Russia and the Mackenzie in Canada.

Gulf of Finland

ESTONIA

The Nordic countries of Denmark, Norway, Sweden, Finland and Iceland are not only surrounded by seas but their interiors too are made up of water—with a multitude of rivers, waterfalls and lakes.

LATVIA

LITHUANIA

The terrifying Midgard Serpent, or Jörmungandr, of Norse mythology is so long that it encircles the world. If it bites its tail it writhes in rage, shaking the earth.

13

North Sea

NETHERLANDS

Rotterdam is Europe's largest port, at the mouth of the Nieuwe Maas, a tributary of the Rhine.

The Ruhr is one of the greatest industrial areas in Europe and takes its name from a tributary of the Rhine.

Ruhr

The legions of the Roman Empire were defeated at the Battle of the Teutoburg Forest in 9 CE. For the following 400 years the Rhine was the border of the Roman Empire.

BELGIUM

Cologne has been inhabited since the Paleolithic Age.

Frankfurt am Main lies on the banks of the river Main. This ages-old city is now a European financial hub.

Moselle

LUXEMBOURG

GERMANY

The Moselle runs through France, Luxembourg and Germany. With a gentle flow and many tributaries, the river is popular for fishing.

Rhine

Main

Europe's biggest waterfall is in Switzerland. The Rhine Falls are 150 m (490 ft) wide and 23 m (75 ft)

The French city of Strasbourg is the seat of the European Parliament.

FRANCE

SWITZERLAND

The Rhine begins at Lake Toma in the Oberalp Pass, then travels through the mountains to vast alpine grasslands.

14

Ships have transported goods on the Rhine since the 13th century, when koffs carried cargo of up to 250 tons. Today's barges on the river can be 130 m (430 ft) long, transporting loads more than ten times that weight.

The **Rhine** has been a vital trade route since Roman times and is linked by canals to other major rivers such as the Danube and the Rhône. The Rhine flows from the Swiss Alps through the valleys, ravines and great plains of France and Germany to reach the Netherlands, where it enters the North Sea. In the Netherlands, the Rhine divides into three main branches forming a complex network of rivers and canals that make up one of Europe's largest river deltas.

In the 1960s the Rhine was so badly polluted that it could hardly sustain life. The water quality has since been improved enough that salmon have returned to the river.

The Lorelei is a steep rock beside the Rhine. According to folklore, there lived a nymph whose singing enchanted passing sailors and lured their ships onto the rocks.

The lammergeier, or bearded vulture, feeds mainly on carcasses. It drops large bones from a great height to break them up.

In Richard Wagner's opera Das Rheingold the daughters of Father Rhine keep watch over the Rhine gold.

15

The source of the Danube is in the Black Forest, which has given rise to many legends, including a deer said to have leapt a vast ravine to escape hunters.

The Danube has long been celebrated in music. The famous waltz *The Blue Danube* (1866) by Johann Strauss the Younger epitomized the atmosphere of imperial Vienna.

GERMANY

CZECH REPUBLI

The region of Regensburg was first inhabited in the Stone Age. Later came Celtic settlements and a Roman fort, after which the town was established.

Vienna, with its many Baroque buildings, is the capital of Austria and a hub of classical music and opera.

Danube

The Romans called this thickly wooded area Silva Nigra, the black forest.

AUSTRIA

Sava

SLOVENIA

CROATIA

Jellyfish tentacles contain nematocysts, which can be fired like arrows to paralyze prey. The tentacles then draw the prey into the mouth.

BOSNIA HERZEGOVI

Most female fish release thousands of eggs into the where they are either eaten by other creatures or feri by male fish. The fertilized eggs develop independently from their parents. Only a few fish species protect their offspring once born or give birth to live young.

Ligurian Sea

Tyrrhenian Sea

ITALY

Adriatic

The Tyrrhenian Sea derives its name from *turrhènoi*, the ancient Greek word for the Etruscans.

16

The **Danube** is Europe's second-longest river after the Volga. It originates in the Black Forest, in the west of Germany, and flows southeast to the Black Sea. The Danube traverses ten countries: Germany, Austria, Slovakia, Hungary, Croatia, Serbia, Romania, Bulgaria, Moldova and Ukraine. It played a crucial role in the establishment and political development of middle and southeast Europe. Many castles and forts were set up on its banks. The river was a border between great kingdoms and cultures, but also a vital trade route. The capital cities Vienna (Austria), Budapest (Hungary) and Belgrade (Serbia)—among others—depended on the Danube for their economic growth. In the 21st century the river remains an important trade artery.

The first towns in Europe were built near the Danube around 5700 BCE. The inhabitants used water from the river for their agriculture.

Environmental disasters have caused great damage to the world's rivers and seas. In 2000 a dam that burst near a gold mine swamped the environs with cyanide-contaminated water. Many creatures died in the Someş, Tisza and Danube rivers.

The Danube Delta Biosphere Reserve is a World Heritage Site inhabited by 300 species of birds and rare mammals. The site is protected by the Ramsar Convention, an intergovernmental treaty protecting wetlands.

Budapest is the capital of Hungary. The name combines Buda and Pest, two towns that were united in 1873.

An enormous rock sculpture of Decebalus, the last king of Dacia (87–106 CE), was commissioned by a businessman in the 1990s and took 10 years to complete.

Between Romania and Serbia there are many narrows, gorges and rapids on the Danube. That part of the river is known as the Iron Gates. It has been easier to navigate since the construction of a flood control dam in the 1960s, when five villages, a town and the island of Ada were inundated.

Galaţi in Romania has the largest port on the Danube.

Belgrade, capital of Serbia, has been destroyed 44 times in 115 wars.

Apollodorus of Damascus, architect for the Roman emperor Trajan, built a stone bridge over the Danube in 103 CE. Trajan's bridge was destroyed by the emperor Aurelian during his retreat in 270 CE.

Shoes on the Danube in Budapest is a memorial to the 3500 people shot by the Arrow Cross, a party sympathetic to Nazi Germany. Sixty pairs of metal shoes symbolize the victims, who had to remove their shoes before they were shot and fell into the Danube.

SLOVAKIA

HUNGARY

ROMANIA

MOLDOVA

UKRAINE

Prut

SERBIA

Olt

Danube

BULGARIA

Black Sea

Piet Hein, privateer and commander of the Dutch West India Company, captured the Spanish treasure fleet in 1628 during the Eighty Years' War.

Seaweed has adapted to life underwater. It is the only flowering plant that lives in the sea and produces pollen, which is circulated by water and small crayfish. In earlier times, large seaweed was used to build dikes.

Pole-vaulting over water is a traditional sport in Friesland dating from when farmers had to leap wide ditches to get from one field to another.

Wadden Sea

IJsselmeer

Markermeer

In the mid-20th century the Zuiderzee was blocked off from the Wadden Sea and turned into a lake, with surrounding land reclaimed.

North Sea

Amsterdam has 165 canals and millions of wooden piles supporting its buildings.

The Delta Works is a system of dams and storm-surge barriers built after a major flood in 1953 to protect the Netherlands from flooding.

IJssel

During the Battle of the Yser in 1914, the sluice gates were opened to hinder the advance of German troops.

Waal

NETHERLANDS

GERMANY

Rhine

Yser

Scheldt

BELGIUM

Lys

There was once a large flax industry on the Lys. The water was low in iron and lime, making it ideal for retting the flax. That process gave the river a golden gleam and the nickname "golden river."

In Flemish legend, the giant Antigoon chopped off the hand of any sailor who refused to pay his toll. The hero Brabo slew the giant, cut off his hand and flung it into the Scheldt. The name Antwerp is derived from the Dutch handen werpen, to throw hands.

Two dragonflies form a mating wheel.

Meuse

In the 16th century the Flemish cartographer Gerardus Mercator pioneered the drawing of maps with the meridians and parallels as straight lines, despite the spherical nature of Earth. Compass directions became truer, even though the appearance of the globe was a little distorted. This remains the most common method of mapmaking.

Belgian fries are the best in the world.

Eels swim from fresh water to the sea to spawn. They can even cross land at night, if it is wet enough.

This tiny wren can sing at 90 decibels.

Most windmills in the Netherlands are used for pumping water. During World War II the Resistance sent coded messages through positioning the windmill vanes.

Herons have patches of powder down, fine feathers with tips that disintegrate into a powder as they grow. The herons use the powder to clean their other feathers.

The **Rhine–Meuse–Scheldt Delta** is the gateway from the North Sea to north and central Europe. Tidal action has widened the river mouths into connected estuaries.

The **Scheldt** begins in the north of France, flows through Belgium and empties into the North Sea via the Netherlands. The Scheldt has three parts: the Upper Scheldt, from its source to Ghent; the Zeeschelde, the busiest stretch between Ghent and Antwerp to the border with the Netherlands; and the West Scheldt, from the border to the river mouth.

The **Meuse** originates on the Langres Plateau in France and runs northwards through France, Belgium and the Netherlands to the North Sea.

The skater can dive, fly and run over water, staying afloat by means of the water-repellent microscopic hairs on its feet and abdomen.

The great diving beetle carries an air bubble under its wings and abdomen so it can breathe.

The water spider lives mostly underwater. Its submerged web contains a large air bubble, which the spider makes by transporting air with the tiny hairs on its abdomen.

19

According to a legend, the Archangel Michael appeared in around 700 CE to the Bishop of Avranches and instructed him to build a chapel on Mont Saint-Michel. Not until his third appearance, when Michael burnt a hole in the bishop's head with his finger, was the bishop finally convinced.

Rollo the Norseman (ca. 860–932) was so large that no horse could carry him. The Viking became ruler of Normandy. In exchange he had to defend the Seine (which gave entry to Paris) against his former fellow-Vikings.

FRANCE

Asterix's village—where brave Gauls defy the invading Romans.

The world's first tidal power station was built in 1966 on the banks of the Rance. The flow of water between high and low tides drove the turbines.

During World War I the city of Tours became an American garrison with 25,000 soldiers. They built textile works, munitions depots, a post office and a hospital.

A German submarine base was built in Lorient during World War II. The French navy used the base after the war, and it is now a museum.

French cargo barges with a collapsible mast were used widely until the arrival of the railways.

Born in Nantes in 1828, Jules Verne was one of the first writers of science fiction, whose books include Twenty Thousand Leagues Under the Sea.

The **Seine**, the best-known river in France, flows from the Langres Plateau near Dijon, north via Troyes and Paris to Rouen, and empties into the Channel at Le Havre. The **Loire** is France's longest river. Its source is in the Cévennes mountains and its upper reaches are fed by melting snow. The river flows from the mountains, northward past Orléans and Nantes, emptying into the Atlantic Ocean at Saint-Nazaire.

Bay of Biscay

No other mammal dives as deep as Cuvier's beaked whale. Its Latin name, Ziphius cavirostris, refers to the fabled animal Ziphius, a kind of aggressive whale-owl.

Landes Forest

Seine

Clovis became the first king of what would later be France in 509. He united the Frankish tribes under one rule and made Paris his capital.

Cenabum was the capital of the Carnutes, a mighty Celtic people who began their uprising against the Roman occupiers here in 53 BCE. The city is now called Orléans.

A large Gallic shrine once stood at the sources of the Seine, and pilgrims visited pagan temples there until the 4th century, when they were closed at the command of the Roman emperor Theodosius.

There are more than 140 chateaus in the Loire Valley, known as the Garden of France.

In the 17th century people thought the waters of the Seine had healing powers. A grotto was built at the main spring, with a statue of Sequana, the goddess who gave her name to the Seine.

Loire

Around 600 BCE the Greeks founded a trading post in present-day Marseille in the south of France, and planted vineyards nearby. The Romans later introduced wine-growing to middle and northern France.

Catherine de' Medici owned a number of the chateaus in the Loire Valley. She was first queen, and later regent, of France in the mid-16th century, and the mother of three French kings.

A tap was put in at the source of the Loire, from which water flows. There is also a spring in a nearby meadow. No one knows which of the two is the true source.

21

The **Po** is Italy's longest river. It begins in the Cottian Alps and flows to the Adriatic Sea via several important Italian cities including Turin, Piacenza and Ferrara. Its catchment is the largest and most fertile plain in Italy. Because the Po is prone to flooding, much of its course is constrained by dikes.

The **Tiber** is the second-longest river in Italy. It rises from two springs on the slopes of Mount Fumaiolo in the Apennines. The Tiber flows southwards through gorges and broad valleys and through Rome, finally reaching the Tyrrhenian Sea via a delta.

Po

ITALY

Ligurian Sea

Tyrrhenian Sea

FRANCE

CORSICA

The Shroud of Turin was said to be the cloth used to wrap Jesus's dead body. Radiocarbon dating shows it is not that old but, as is often the case with relics, not everyone agrees.

The Taurini, a Celtic people, were the first to settle near Turin. Later, the town became a Roman army camp, a trading post in the Middle Ages, the headquarters of the noble House of Savoy and the first capital of a united Italy.

Piacenza was heavily bombed by Allied forces during World War II to prevent supplies getting through to Germany's retreating forces.

Fish take in oxygen by letting water pass through their gills. Gills are made up of hundreds of small plates full of fine blood vessels.

While most fish have a protective gill cover, rays and sharks have gill-slits instead.

When flatfish are young, they have eyes on both sides of their head. As they grow, the lower eye moves towards the upper eye, so they can use both eyes to look up from the sea floor.

During the siege of Rome by the Goths in 537–8, General Belisarius used ship mills on the Tiber to continue grinding corn. They were invented by the Roman engineer and architect Vitruvius.

Megalithic standing stones erected around 1500 BCE stand by the Taravo River in Filitosa.

In 1863 the Corsican chemist Angelo Mariani brewed a drink with a base of coca extract and Bordeaux wine and exported it to America. There, pharmacist John Pemberton adapted his own versions, eventually making a non-alcoholic drink he called Coca-Cola.

The city of Venice is built on 118 small islands in a lagoon. In around 700 Venice appointed a duke and became the Republic of Venice, remaining an economic power until 1797.

Gulf of Trieste

Venice

Venetian Lagoon

Bivalves and snails have shells made of lime, which they produce themselves.

Nudibranchs are a type of sea slug known for their bizarre and bright forms.

The House of Este, a princely dynasty from Ferrara, was known in the Renaissance for its patronage of the arts and learning.

Leonardo da Vinci, the Italian Renaissance artist and genius, was fascinated by water and rivers. He designed bridges, tunnels, canals, pumps and even a kind of diving suit.

The Mediterranean scallop has photo-sensitive organs along the edge of its shell. If these "eyes" detect danger it quickly shuts its shell, which makes it spring backwards.

Adriatic Sea

Tiber

Rome

3000-year-old Rome is the Eternal City, the cradle of Roman civilization, the capital of Italy. In Rome lies the Vatican, the world's smallest nation and home to the Pope.

According to Roman myth, twins Romulus and Remus were placed in a reed basket in the Tiber. Found and raised by a wolf, they went on to establish Rome.

Spaghetti alle vongole is a popular Italian pasta dish made with clams.

23

Spiny lobsters migrate during the winter to deeper, warmer water, marching in lines of 50 or more.

Fish consume water through osmosis so have adapted to maintain a balance of salt in their bodies relative to the water in which they swim. Saltwater fish have a low concentration of salt in their bloodstream, so must drink a lot to maintain blood, with a high salt level in their blood. Freshwater fish are the opposite: with a high salt level in their blood, they drink little and expel excess water quickly.

Sponges are simple invertebrates, without organs. They are made up of various cells, each with a unique function—structure, reproduction or nutrition. Sponges filter food from water. Most live in the sea though some can be found in fresh water.

They may have been the first animals on Earth.

Sponges are very absorbent. They were used by ancient Greeks for polishing and as paint brushes. Roman soldiers drank from them.

The Portuguese poet Fernando Pessoa wrote the poem "The Tagus is lovelier than the river flowing through my village" in 1914.

"My hair turns white but the Tagus is forever young" are the lyrics of a popular Fado song.

North Atlantic Ocean

The Roman arched bridge of Alcántara was completed in 106 CE, but later damaged during various conflicts, due to its strategic position.

PORTO

Lisbon, the capital of Portugal, is one of Europe's oldest cities, existing since 1200 BCE.

PORTUGAL

Sea urchins are spiny-coated invertebrates. Their eating mechanism is called "Aristotle's Lantern," after the Greek philosopher who described them in his History of the Animals.

The Algarve is famous as the place where fossils of the Miocene sea eagles were found and is a paradise for fossil hunters.

In July 1497 Vasco da Gama left Lisbon on a voyage of exploration. His journeys opened the sea route to India.

The **Tagus** is the longest river on the Iberian Peninsula. It begins in the Muela de San Juan mountain, to the east of Madrid, and runs westwards through Spain and Portugal to the Atlantic Ocean via an estuary at Lisbon. Its upper reaches flow through small, winding valleys and deep gorges and ravines. In Toledo, the Tagus joins the Guadarrama. The Tagus is navigable from Santarém, Portugal. The river supplies drinking water to the greater part of central Spain and Portugal, and dozens of hydro power plants along the river generate electricity.

Extra-thick bone and shock-absorbing muscles protect the skull of the great spotted woodpecker, which pecks a tree more than 10 times per second in search of insects.

Pine tree seeds

The Iberian wall lizard is a reptile, as are snakes, tortoises and crocodiles. These cold-blooded animals have scales and no larval stage.

According to legend, a girl from Carrovillas de Alconétar was bewitched by her mother and now lives as a mermaid in the Alcántara Dam. At full moon she enchants and drowns her victims.

The Jarama and Tagus rivers merge in Aranjuez, close to Madrid.

Toledo, famous for sword-making since the 5th century, was built on a mountaintop beside the Tagus.

Tagus

Alcántara Dam, one of the largest reservoirs in Europe, was built in 1969.

SPAIN

The Iberian newt is an amphibian: a cold-blooded creature that can live on water and on land. Other amphibians include frogs and salamanders. The newt's skin lets in both water and oxygen. Its early life is spent underwater as a larva but it does not live in the sea. Because seawater contains more salt than the newt's blood, it would lose too much fluid through its thin skin and dry out.

Al-Bakri was a geographer and historian from Al-Andalus, present-day Spain. He wrote The Book of Roads and Kingdoms in 1068 without ever leaving his native land. He compiled this important historical work about African and Arabian trade routes from stories and reports from traders and explorers.

25

The heavily fished red king crab grows up to 2 m (6½ ft) across.

Bering Sea

Yukon

Sea of Okhotsk

During the Ice Age, Alaska and Siberia were joined by a land bridge across the Bering Sea. It is considered likely that the first modern humans reached America 12,000 years ago via this bridge.

Gulf of Alaska

Unhcegila, a giant serpent from Lakota mythology, rose from the sea to visit death and destruction on the Black Hills. Fabulous serpents, some with horns, appear often in the stories of Native Americans.

Plastic and other human debris carried by the great ocean currents has gathered into several huge gyres. This plastic soup in the Pacific Ocean was discovered by a sailor in 1997. It covers an area at least as large as the country of Chile, some say as large as Antarctica.

North
Pacific Ocean

Hawai'i

Great white sharks are the largest predatory fish in the world, some longer than 6 m (20 ft). Great whites live in all the oceans and can travel up to 150 km (90 mi) per day.

NORTH AMERICA

Three-quarters of the world's polar bears live in Canada.

Northwest Passage

Hudson Bay

Canada

United States

...down to the river...

Gulf of Saint Lawrence

Hudson

Missouri

Colorado

Mississippi

Rio Grande

Gulf of California

Mexico

Gulf of Mexico

Caribbean Sea

Many ships and planes have vanished mysteriously in the Bermuda Triangle. Possible scientific explanations include high traffic density, gigantic waves, disturbances in the magnetic field and high concentrations of methane.

Arribada (Spanish for **arrival**) is the period when a huge number of female dwarf turtles come to lay their eggs on the beaches of Mexico and Costa Rica.

27

The **Yukon** is one of North America's longest rivers. It originates near Tagish Lake in the Canadian territory of British Columbia. It flows in a northwesterly direction through the territory of Yukon, Alaska, emptying into the Bering Sea. The Yukon was the most important transport route in the region until the 1950s, when the Alaska Highway was completed. With global warming, the Kaskawulsh glacier continues to retreat, changing the course of several rivers. The meltwater originally flowed through the Slims River to the Bering Sea, but now flows via the Alsek to the Gulf of Alaska. This change happened very suddenly in 2016.

A large part of Alaska is tundra, a cold, polar region with no trees. Instead, mosses, grasses and shrubs grow here.

The Yukon has the world's longest salmon run. The full-grown chum salmon swim as far as 3000 km (1900 mi) upstream to their spawning ground.

Tanana

The wood frog freezes for seven months over winter, then it thaws out and life goes on.

Bering Sea

A council of 70 groups of indigenous peoples of Alaska and Canada aims to improve the water quality of the Yukon.

More than 40% of all Alaskans live in Anchorage. The city grew after the arrival of the railway in 1914 and again when oil was discovered in 1968.

Barnacles are crustaceans. As larvae they fasten onto places such as tidal rocks, ships' hulls and whales. The small creatures build houses out of lime and put out their feet to grab food.

ALASKA

Alaska was sold to the United States by Russia in 1867. It is the largest US state but also the most sparsely populated.

Sea otters live on shellfish, sea urchins, crabs and lobsters. If they can't open a shell they lay a stone on their bellies and break the shell on it.

The 3 m (10 ft) long left tooth of the male narwhal is a sensory organ, able to detect temperature and the chemical make-up of water.

Shelikof Strait

Kodiak Archipelago

Alaskan grizzly bears are larger than their counterparts in the Rocky Mountains because of their diet of fatty salmon.

Yukon

When a steamboat ran aground in 1901, gold prospectors on board convinced the merchant accompanying them to set up a trading post, so establishing Fairbanks, now Alaska's largest inland city.

Wrangell–Saint Elias is the largest national park in the United States, with an area of over 50,000 km² (20,000 mi²).

Mount Saint Elias

During the gold rush of 1896–99, more than 100,000 prospectors searched for gold in Klondike on the Yukon. Dawson, a town of 500, grew by 30,000 within two years.

CANADA

...aska natives and Europeans first came into contact in 1741.

When orcas rest they stay alert by letting each half of their brain sleep in turn.

Gulf of Alaska

The Mahican are the original people of the Hudson Valley. They called the river Mahicannituck or "river that moves in two directions."

Mohawk

The Mohawk, named after the Mohawk Nation, is the largest tributary of the Hudson.

Albany, the capital of New York State, was founded in 1614 as Fort Nassau, a trading post where beaver skins were bought from the native inhabitants.

UNITED STATES OF AMERICA

Ida Lewis was a lighthouse keeper on Rhode Island famous for her multiple sea rescues. Her first was in 1854 at the age of 12.

Dutch colonists established New Netherland in 1624, calling the Hudson North River. The capital was New Amsterdam, present-day Manhattan in New York City.

British Henry Hudson explored on behalf of the Dutch East India Company, a trading enterprise which named the Hudson River after him. During his fourth voyage to Hudson Bay (also named after him) in 1611, a mutiny broke out. Hudson and some others were abandoned in a small boat and never heard from again. The crew sailed the ship back to England.

Hudson

Petrus Stuyvesant was the last director-general of New Netherland, until its conquest by the English in 1664.

Italian explorer Giovanni da Verrazzano was the first European to sail into Upper New York Bay in 1524.

The **Hudson** begins in the Adirondack Mountains in the north of New York State. The river flows via Albany to New York City and on into the North Atlantic Ocean. The Erie Canal links the Hudson with Lake Erie and therefore the Atlantic Ocean with the Great Lakes—five large lakes on the border of the United States and Canada. Once the Erie Canal was completed in 1825, it became an important traffic route, allowing settlers to travel deep inland from New York.

The One World Trade Center is the tallest building on the American continent.

In 1933 King Kong made the first ascent of the Empire State Building.

In 1913 the Woolworth Building was the tallest building on Earth.

In 2009, US Airways Flight 1549 made a successful emergency landing on the Hudson.

...ose but its light was too weak.

The light installation Tribute in Light is turned on annually on 9/11.

Brooklyn Bridge was built in 1883.

Manhattan is an island and one of five boroughs of New York. The island is surrounded by the East, the Harlem and the Hudson rivers.

Missouri

The new migrants brought many new animals and plants with them to America from Europe, but they also brought diseases. A great many indigenous people died. By the start of the 19th century, more than half of the Plains Indians had died of smallpox.

Rafting was used to transport wood. Huge temporary rafts were constructed from tree trunks and floated downriver.

In the 19th century the Missouri was one of the most important transport routes for the western expansion of the United States.

The American bison is the largest mammal in North America, weighing up to a ton.

The Great Plains is a vast stretch of land between the Rocky Mountains and the Mississippi, from Texas to beyond the Canadian border. It was originally prairie grasslands.

UNITED STATES OF AMERICA

The large wooden steamboats on the Mississippi played a considerable role in developing the river's economic importance. The journey from St. Louis to New Orleans, which used to take three months, could be completed in four days by steamboat.

Mark Twain, author of The Adventures of Tom Sawyer and The Adventures of Huckleberry Finn, wrote about life on the Mississippi in the late 19th century. He was a steamboat pilot and took his pseudonym from the measurement that people regularly called out while plumbing the depths of the river—mark twain, meaning mark number two.

MEXICO

The **Mississippi** begins in Lake Itasca, in the north of the state of Minnesota, then meanders gently south to the Gulf of Mexico. The upper reaches contain many dams and locks, built during the 1930s and 1940s. Because of the tributaries that flow into the Mississippi, it grows ever wider, especially after it meets the **Missouri**, its most important tributary. When Europeans first explored and claimed parts of America, they used the rivers as convenient borders between colonies, such as New Spain and New France. Later the Mississippi and Missouri rivers were used by settlers moving inland as the US government killed and forcibly relocated Native Americans so the land could be sold to others.

Lake Superior

There are approximately 35,000 islands in the Great Lakes.

CANADA

Lake Huron

Lake Michigan

Lake Ontario

Lake Erie

St. Anthony Falls is the only true waterfall on the Mississippi River. Although sacred to the Dakota Indians, it was used by settlers to power the lumber and flour mills that began the city of Minneapolis.

In 2012 a 125-year-old sturgeon was caught in a small river by the Great Lakes that weighed 109 kg (240 lb) and was over 2 m (6½ ft) long.

The Niagara Falls consists of three waterfalls, one of them partly in Canada.

Mississippi

Ohio

A distillery in the Appalachian Mountains, in which moonshine or alcohol (often illegal) is home-made.

Kansas City, the city with many fountains.

St. Louis was founded by French fur traders.

Traces of human habitation 8500–14,000 years old have been found beside the Mississippi, Comite and Amite rivers.

Stax

Memphis is named after the capital of ancient Egypt.

During the period before the American Civil War, New Orleans was the country's largest slave market.

North Atlantic Ocean

Red River

New Orleans is the birthplace of jazz.

Mahi-mahi

Hurricane Katrina was responsible for many deaths in 2005. Hardest-hit New Orleans was evacuated.

Gulf of Mexico

33

Roadrunners are considered by many Pueblo tribes to have protective powers.

The Great Salt Lake is a remnant of the prehistoric Lake Bonneville that once covered a large part of North America.

The Golden Gate Bridge in San Francisco is named for the Golden Gate Strait which it spans.

Sierra Nevada

There are more than 100 casinos and approximately 125,000 hotel rooms in Las Vegas. Its millions of lights make it the brightest place on Earth.

The Grand Canyon is a deep ravine cut by the Colorado river through northwestern Arizona.

A male humpback whale can sing for days on end in the mating season.

HOLLYWOOD

Lake Mead

Hoover Dam

Death Valley in the Mojave Desert is the hottest place in the western hemisphere. In summer, temperatures can exceed 50 °C (120 °F).

Pacific Ocean

Gulf of California

UNITED STATES
OF AMERICA

Salt Lake

According to the Mojave, the original people of the Mojave Desert, the river was created by the son of their own creator, Mastamho.

Colorado

Denver lies exactly one mile above sea level. That is why it's sometimes called the Mile High City.

Rocky Mountains

Lake Powell

...shoe Bend: the horseshoe-shaped ...er loop below the Glen Canyon Dam.

Mesa Verde National Park contains more than 4300 archaeological sites, 600 of them cliff dwellings. The area was settled by the Ancestral Pueblo people 1400 years ago.

According to stories, a UFO crashed near Roswell, New Mexico, in 1947.

The **Colorado** begins in the high Rocky Mountains in the state of Colorado. It flows through the states of Utah, Arizona, Nevada and California, then along the border between the United States and Mexico. From there it empties into the Gulf of California. Hardly any water from the Colorado reaches the sea, since nearly all of it is used for irrigation or drinking water.

Historically people have crossed the border and the Rio Grande River, looking for work in America.

MEXICO

Guatemala

El Salvador

Deep-sea anglers live in the dark. The smaller, weaker male searches for a female mate using his sense of smell. When he finds one, he bites her and his mouth fuses with her body. Their bloodstreams become connected and the male lives permanently on his mate as a parasite.

Charles Darwin's observations on the Galapagos Islands in 1835 helped him develop his theory of evolution.

Female deep-sea anglers lure their prey with a "lamp" of luminous bacteria.

The gulper eel is a deep-sea fish that can swallow prey larger than itself.

The barreleye has a belly that can light up, making it almost invisible to predators below as it doesn't show against the bright surface of the water.

Mutineers from HMS *Bounty* went ashore on Pitcairn Island.

Easter Island is famous for its moai— massive human figures—set into the ground.

South Pacific Ocean

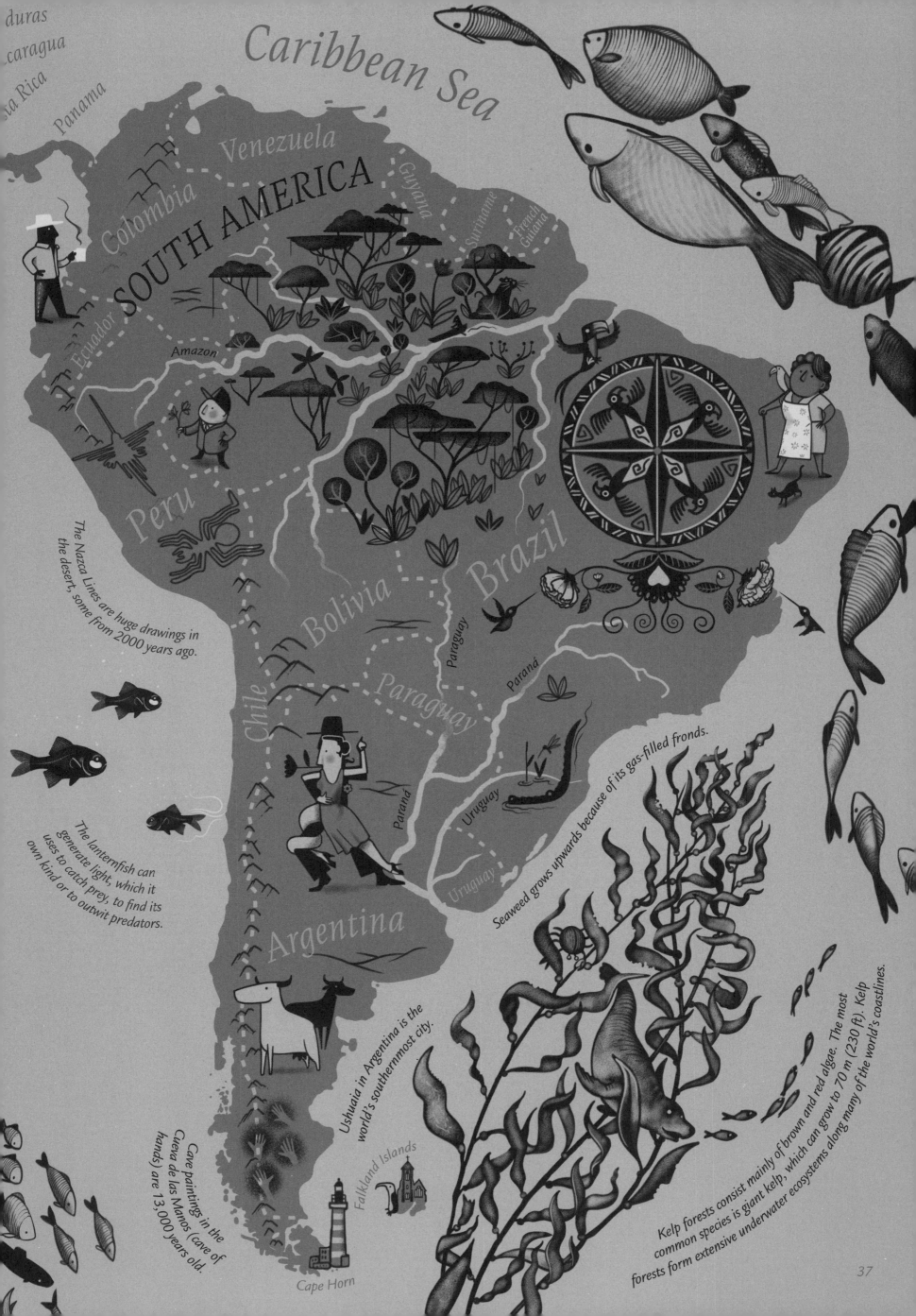

duras

caragua

a Rica

Panama

Caribbean Sea

Venezuela

Colombia

Guyana

Suriname

French Guiana

SOUTH AMERICA

Ecuador

Amazon

Peru

Brazil

Bolivia

Paraguay

Paraguay

Parana

Paraná

Uruguay

Uruguay

Chile

Paraguay

Paraná

Argentina

Falkland Islands

Cape Horn

The Nazca Lines are huge drawings in the desert, some from 2000 years ago.

The lanternfish can generate light, which it uses to catch prey, to find its own kind or to outwit predators.

Ushuaia in Argentina is the world's southernmost city.

Cave paintings in the Cueva de las Manos (cave of hands) are 13,000 years old.

Seaweed grows upwards because of its gas-filled fronds.

Kelp forests consist mainly of brown and red algae. The most common species is giant kelp, which can grow to 70 m (230 ft). Kelp forests form extensive underwater ecosystems along many of the world's coastlines.

VENEZUELA

COLOMBIA

Boa constrictor

Black jaguar

EQUADOR

Rio Negro

Iquitos, with more than 400,000 inhabitants, is the largest city in the world that is accessible only by air or water.

Howler monkey

Sloth

PERU

The Amazon forest is sometimes called the lungs of the world. It produces about 20% of all the world's oxygen.

South Pacific Ocean

GUYANA

SURINAME

FRENCH GUIANA

North Atlantic Ocean

Nearly one-fifth of all the world's river water flowing into the sea comes from the Amazon. Its flow is so strong that early sailors found they could drink its fresh water while still far offshore.

Amazon Arena

Anteater

Amazon

At the end of the 19th century, Manaus was the wealthy hub of the rubber trade.

The pororoca is a tidal bore. At high tide, the sea surges inland, taking waves as high as 4 m (13 ft) up the Amazon.

The busy trade and port city of Belém is the entryway to the Amazon.

BRAZIL

Large parts of the rainforest are being cut down to produce wood and paper, with soya and palm oil plantations, and mines, taking its place.

The **Amazon** begins in the Peruvian Andes, flows northeast through Brazil and empties into the Atlantic Ocean at the equator. The river has more than 1110 tributaries and carries the greatest water volume of any river in the world. Water is life, and in the rainforests of the Amazon basin live millions of insects, hundreds of thousands of plant species and thousands of species of birds and mammals. The river's length is disputed as there are two possible sources. The river is at least 6259 km (3889 mi) long, probably the longest in the world after the Nile.

Electric eels can deliver a shock of more than 650 volts to stun prey or ward off predators.

Bolivia

BRAZIL

The capybara is the world's largest rodent. Its nose, ears and eyes are at the top of its head so it can hide in water.

Paraguay

Paraná

ANDES MOUNTAINS

PARAGUAY

ARGENTINA

The Itaipu Dam is the second-largest dam in the world and has the highest energy output.

Paraná

An underwater ravine in the Uruguay River is 100 m (330 ft) deeper in places than the rest of the riverbed. The Yucumá, or Moconá, waterfall runs parallel to the river and plunges into the ravine.

Uruguay

The Mapuche were the original inhabitants of central and southern Chile and southern Argentina. Like other cultures, the Mapuche have a flood myth in which the world is destroyed and recreated.

Buenos Aires is the capital of Argentina.

URUGUAY

The flower of the cockspur coral tree is the national flower of Uruguay and Argentina.

CHILE

Brazil's capital Brasília was built in the 1950s.

The Rio de Janeiro carnival lasts five days. Every year someone is appointed King Momo to lead the festivities.

More than 12 million people live in São Paulo, the largest metropolis in the Americas.

The female seahorse lays her eggs in the male's brood pouch and the male hatches the eggs.

Silky sharks scrape against gigantic whale sharks to loosen parasites from their skin.

South Atlantic Ocean

The Portuguese man o' war is very poisonous and owes its name to explorers who found it as fearsome as the infamous Portuguese warships. It is a siphonophore: not a jellyfish but a collection of polyps, each with its own function.

The **Paraná** is the second-longest river in South America after the Amazon. It begins at the confluence of the Paranaíba and Rio Grande rivers in Central Brazil. From there it flows south, merging with first the Paraguay and then the **Uruguay**, before entering the Atlantic Ocean. The Paraná's catchment of about 2,800,000 km² (1,100,000 mi²) includes parts of Brazil, Paraguay, Bolivia and Argentina. The Paraná and the Uruguay together form a vast river mouth, the **Río de la Plata**, about 220 km (140 mi) wide at the Atlantic Ocean.

Barents Sea

Kara Sea

ASIA

Arthropods make up most of the species in the animal kingdom. These cold-blooded creatures have jointed legs and an exoskeleton of chitin. Insects, arachnids and crustaceans are all arthropods.

Russia

Ambulocetus, a forerunner of the whale, had legs and lived during the Eocene, 40–50 million years ago.

Kazakhstan

Mongolia

Uzbekistan

Georgia

Kyrgyzstan

Caspian Sea

Armenia

Azerbaijan

Turkey

Turkmenistan

Tajikistan

Syria

Tigris

Iran

Afghanistan

Iraq

Euphrates

Pakistan

Nepal

Bhutan

Yellow River

China

Indus

Kuwait

Bangladesh

Yangtze

Saudi Arabia

Ganges

India

Myanmar

Vietnam

United Arab Emirates

Laos

Oman

Flamingo

Bay of Bengal

Thailand

Mekong

Cambodia

Yemen

Andaman Sea

Gulf of Thailand

Sout

Arabian Sea

Laptev Sea

East Siberian Sea

Russia

Lena

In Japanese mythology earthquakes were caused by a gigantic catfish, Namazu, which was guarded and controlled by the god Kashima.

Japanese spider crabs have the longest legs of any arthropod. They can span more than 4 m (13 ft).

The kappa is a mythical water spirit that lives in Japan's rivers and lakes.

Sea of Okhotsk

Sea of Japan

North Korea

South Korea

Yellow Sea

Japan

At the start of the 15th century the Chinese Admiral Zheng He commanded the largest armada in the world. With his 62 large ships and 200 small ships, he led expeditions to Africa, among other places.

In Chinese mythology, the dragon kings were tasked with ruling the four seas around China.

There are around 60 species of sea snake in the seas of South East Asia. These venomous snakes can stay underwater for hours with a single breath.

Taiwan

East China Sea

Philippine Sea

Ama are Japanese pearl divers, most of them women, who free-dive up to 25 m (80 ft) deep in cold water and can hold their breath for two minutes.

Philippines

43

The sources of the Tigris and the Euphrates are in the Turkish Taurus Mountains, where it is often stormy and thundery. The Syrians' temples to the storm god, portrayed as a bull or taurus, gave the mountains their name.

A kuphar is a traditional round boat made from willow branches and animal skins.

Because of its ethnic diversity and strategic importance, the Iraqi city of Mos... for centuries been subject to wars and destructi...

The mangar, a rare carp found only in the Tigris and Euphrates, can grow as long as 2 m (6½ ft).

Assyrian chariot

SYRIA

Euphrates

The streams that meet to form the Tigris begin in the Taurus Mountains in the east of Turkey. The river flows southeast, along the border of Syria and through Iraq. The Euphrates, west of the Tigris, runs in the same direction and is southwestern Asia's longest river. The two rivers meet in marshland near the port city of Basra, in southern Iraq. They combine to form the Shatt al-Arab, which flows into the Persian Gulf. The fertile area between the Tigris and the Euphrates was called Mesopotamia—the land between two rivers—home to one of the first known civilizations. The river's silt deposits make the ground extremely fertile.

SAUDI ARABIA

According to Greek mythology, Oceanus, the god of the ocean, and Tethys, the goddess of underground rivers and the sea, had 6000 children. The 3000 daughters each controlled a sea or lake. The 3000 sons ruled over the rivers. The god of the Euphrates was called...Euphrates.

Anahita is an ancient Persian goddess of water, fertility, healing and wisdom.

IRAN

IRAQ

According to a Sumerian epic, the inhabitants of Uruk altered the course of the Euphrates so they could bury their godlike king and hero Gilgamesh beneath the riverbed.

The Tigris is deeper than the Euphrates, so it is more easily navigable and therefore of greater economic importance.

Baghdad is one of the hottest cities in the world with summer temperatures averaging 44 °C (111 °F).

Sinbad the sailor, a fabled character from One Thousand and One Nights, left the port of Basra in search of adventure.

Tigris

Babylon was an enormous city that straddled the Euphrates. Mention of it was found on a 4500-year-old clay tablet.

According to the Bible story, after the great flood, people all spoke the same language and settled in Sumer, the southernmost part of Mesopotamia. They tried to build a mighty tower that would reach heaven — the Tower of Babel. Angered, God made them all speak in different languages. They no longer understood one another and dispersed across the world.

KUWAIT

PERSIAN GULF

Codfish

Barents Sea

Kara Sea

The whistling hare builds large bales of hay for its winter supply.

In the north of Siberia nomads still live by keeping reindeer, fishing and hunting.

Millions of people died in the punishment and work camps of the former Soviet Union. In these gulags (named after the government department responsible, the Gulag) people worked in mines and factories. Conditions were harsh and the camps were set in desolate and distant places.

Migratory birds winter over in the south, away from their breeding grounds and the icy cold.

Sakha is the largest region of Russia. The start of summer is celebrated each year during the Sakha Festival. The Sakha, or Yakut, people greet the sun, dance the Ohuokhai and drink kumis, fermented horse milk.

The small and sturdy Yakutian horse can find grass even under a thick layer of snow and survive in temperatures as low as -45 °C (-49 °F).

In the east of Russia's Siberia, the **Lena** is one of the longest rivers in the world. From Lake Baikal it flows to the north via the Lena Delta to the Laptev Sea, part of the Arctic Ocean. The Lena is 95% meltwater and rain, with little flow in winter when the river freezes. There is much flooding in summer as the melting snow seeks its way to the sea. Lena means "great river." In the west of Siberia, the Ob river flows northwest into the Arctic, draining a basin of nearly 3,000,000 km² (1,150,000 mi²). It is the world's seventh-longest river and was an important transport route until the Trans-Siberian Railway was completed in 1916.

KAZAKHSTAN

The Lena Delta Wildlife Reserve is one of the largest nature reserves in Russia. It lies above the Arctic Circle and is covered in snow for most of the year.

Laptev Sea

Arctic fox

When the ice begins to melt in spring, it can break apart spectacularly, forming walls of ice downstream.

The Lena Pillars are gigantic, naturally created rock formations on the banks of the Lena. They were formed more than 500 million years ago during the Cambrian period, or Cambrian Explosion, when many multi-cellular creatures came into being in a short time. The pillars contain many fossils from that period.

...erryboats can't operate because of the ice in winter so people drive on the rivers instead.

RUSSIA

Yakutsk is the biggest port on the Lena and the capital of Sakha. Its Melnikov Permafrost Institute has been researching the world's coldest places for over 50 years.

Lena

Russians did not start exploring Siberia until the 16th century.

Lake Baikal

Lake Baikal is the largest freshwater reservoir in the world and the deepest lake.

The Olonkho are heroic poems of the Yakut. They can have over 20,000 verses and are performed by a singing storyteller. Every community has its own storyteller, with a repertoire of epic tales about warriors, gods, animals and even modern-day events.

MONGOLIA

CHINA

47

In the Indus Valley, archaeologists have found more than 1000 sites of the Harappa Culture from the Bronze Age.

Islamabad was built in the 1960s as the new capital of Pakistan.

AFGHANISTAN

Indus

The fertile Punjab area, irrigated by five rivers, is the granary of India and Pakistan.

Brahminy kite

PAKISTAN

The Indus Valley linked east and west via trade routes. The area was of strategic and economic importance and many people vied to control it.

Karachi was formerly a coastal town with a few thousand inhabitants. Today it is one of the biggest cities in the world, with more than 21 million people.

In 1947, following the end of British rule in India, the huge land mass was divided into India and Pakistan: one state for Hindus and the other for Muslims.

INDIA

The gharial has 106–110 teeth—more than any other crocodile. It eats only fish.

The black marlin lives in the sea and hunts other fish. It can reach speeds of 130 kmph (80 mph).

Arabian Sea

The Manthoka Waterfall in Skardu, Pakistan.

...erfalls are formed when water flows from hard rock onto soft. The soft rock wears away increasing the difference in height. They can also be formed more quickly by the movement of underground plates or volcanic activity.

Mount Kailash, the source of the Indus, is an important place of pilgrimage for Buddhists and Hindus. According to Hindus, the mountaintop is the home of Shiva and his wife Parvati. According to Buddhists, the Buddha Chakrasamvara is there.

Pilgrims of different religions walk together around the mountain.

The **Indus** begins in the Himalayas in Tibet and crosses the mountain range via deep gorges to the Indus Plain. In the Punjab, five tributaries—the Jhelum, Chenab, Ravi, Beas and Sutlej—converge with meltwater from the Himalayas, greatly increasing the size of the Indus. It flows on through the Sindh province and finally reaches the Arabian Sea via the Indus Delta.

In Hindu mythology, Manu is the ancestor of humanity. Following a command from Matsya, the first incarnation of the god Vishnu, Manu built a boat, saving all species of seed and seven prophets from the deluge.

New Delhi is the capital city of India, with more than 26 million inhabitants.

According to Hindu myth, the goddess Ganga streams to Earth via the hair of the god Shiva.

The yeti, or Abominable Snowman, supposedly l the Himalayan mo

NEPAL

In the 3rd century BCE the Ganges River dolphin received special status from Asoka the Great, ruler of the Maurya Empire, so becoming one of the first protected species in history.

The Shah Jahan, fifth ruler of the Mughal Empire, built the Taj Mahal in 1632 on the banks of the Yamuna in Agra, as the final resting place of his beloved wife. The Yamuna is the largest tributary of the Ganges.

Ghats are large steps on the banks of the Ganges where Hindus worship the river goddess Ganga. By washing themselves in the holy river, Hindus purify their souls. When a Hindu person dies, they are usually cremated and their ashes are scattered in the river.

Yamuna

INDIA

Holi Phagwa is a Hindu spring festival celebrating the triumph of good over evil

The Ganges is considered the heart of Indian life, culture and tradition. It runs southeast through a fertile catchment basin. The Ganges is made up of several rivers that begin in the Himalayas. In Hindustan culture the source of the Bhagirathi is considered the source of the Ganges. From the mountains, the Ganges reaches the city of Haridwar, one of the seven most sacred places for Hindus, before flowing on to the Indus-Ganga Plain. Along the way, many tributaries join the Ganges before it reaches the Bay of Bengal via a vast delta.

At 8848 m (29,029 ft), Mount Everest is the highest mountain in the world, astride the border between Nepal and Tibet.

Kathmandu is the capital of Nepal.

To curb pollution, a court in the State of Uttarakhand has given the Ganges the same legal rights as a person. To pollute the river is to injure it, and now this is legally the same as injuring a person.

BHUTAN

Mugger crocodile

Brahmaputra

BANGLADESH

A male Indian bullfrog.

Padma

Ganges

Varanasi, or Benares, by the Ganges is one of the oldest cities in the world. Traces of settlements nearly 4000 years old have been discovered. Varanasi is an important religious site, full of temples, mosques and ghats. This is where the Buddha is said to have given his first sermon, so establishing Buddhism in 528 BCE.

Kolkata, formerly Calcutta, on the Hooghly, a river in the Ganges Delta.

Some species of fish swim in shoals to keep each other company and to confuse their enemies.

The Sundarbans are the largest mangrove forests in the world. Part of the forest is a national park, a protected environment for Bengal tigers.

Bay of Bengal

51

The Great Wall was built to protect the Chinese Empire from invasion by people from the steppes. The wall consists of several defensive walls, with a total length of 21,196 km (13,170 mi).

150,000 years ago, Qinghai Lake was still connected to the Yellow River. This saltwater lake is the largest in China.

According to Chinese books The Classic of Mountains and Seas and The Book of Documents, the legendary ruler Yu the Great (ca. 2200 BCE) was able to control the flooding of the Yellow River by building dams and canals.

The Terracotta Army, about 8000 statues buried in the grave of the first emperor of China, Qin Shi Huang.

Throughout history, the Yellow River has regularly flooded. Millions have died during these floods and ensuing famines.

The Chinese river dolphin, or baiji, was worshipped as the goddess of the river.

CHINA

INDIA

MYANMAR

Mekong

Yangtze

Beijing is the capital of China.

Bohai Sea

Yellow River

More than 24 million people live in Shanghai, the second-largest city in China. It is also the world's busiest port, with over 700 million tons of goods shipped from the port each year.

The Chinese paddlefish grew to 7 m (23 ft) in length but is now possibly extinct.

Dishu is a form of calligraphy on the ground, using water and a large brush. It began in the 1990s in a park in Beijing and can now be found all over China.

's Three Gorges Dam is one of the world's biggest hydroelectric wer plants. It was completed in 2012, 80 years after work began. Flooding the huge area of the reservoir meant relocating 1.24 million people to new homes.

The **Yellow River**, or **Huang He**, begins in the Tibetan Highlands in the Chinese province of Qinghai and flows fast through deep mountain gorges to the Loess Plateau. The river owes its name to its muddy, yellow water. The lower reaches flow in an easterly direction via the Chinese lowlands to the Yellow Sea, which is part of the Pacific Ocean.

The **Yangtze**, **Blue River** or **Chang Jiang**, is the longest river in Asia. It is the third-longest river in the world, after the Nile and the Amazon. A large portion of the river flows through the Tibetan mountains, after which it goes by way of the Yangtze Plain, the "land of rivers and lakes." More than 700 streams and rivers feed into the Yangtze, before it flows into the East China Sea near Shanghai.

Yellow Sea

Snow leopard

The Mekong, Yangtze and Yellow rivers all begin in Sanjiangyuan, an area in the Tibetan Highlands that became China's first protected national park.

Fish can smell underwater. As the water goes through their nostrils and past the olfactory organs, they pick up the scent of food and other fish.

Fish can hear. They have an inner ear by which they keep their balance and receive sound waves.

Fish can move their eyes independently of each other.

INDIA

The largest species of catfish in the world lives in the Mekong. It is threatened with extinction.

CHINA

Hanoi is the capital of Vietnam.

VIETNAM

Mekong

The shell of Cantor's giant softshell turtle is leathery. This shy animal lives in rivers, where it submerges itself to watch for prey.

MYANMAR

THAILAND

Bangkok is the capital of Thailand.

LAOS

Millions of people in the lower Mekong basin make a living from fishing.

Ho Chi Minh City, formerly called Saigon.

Tonlé Sap Lake

CAMBODIA

Bay of Bengal

Gulf of Thailand

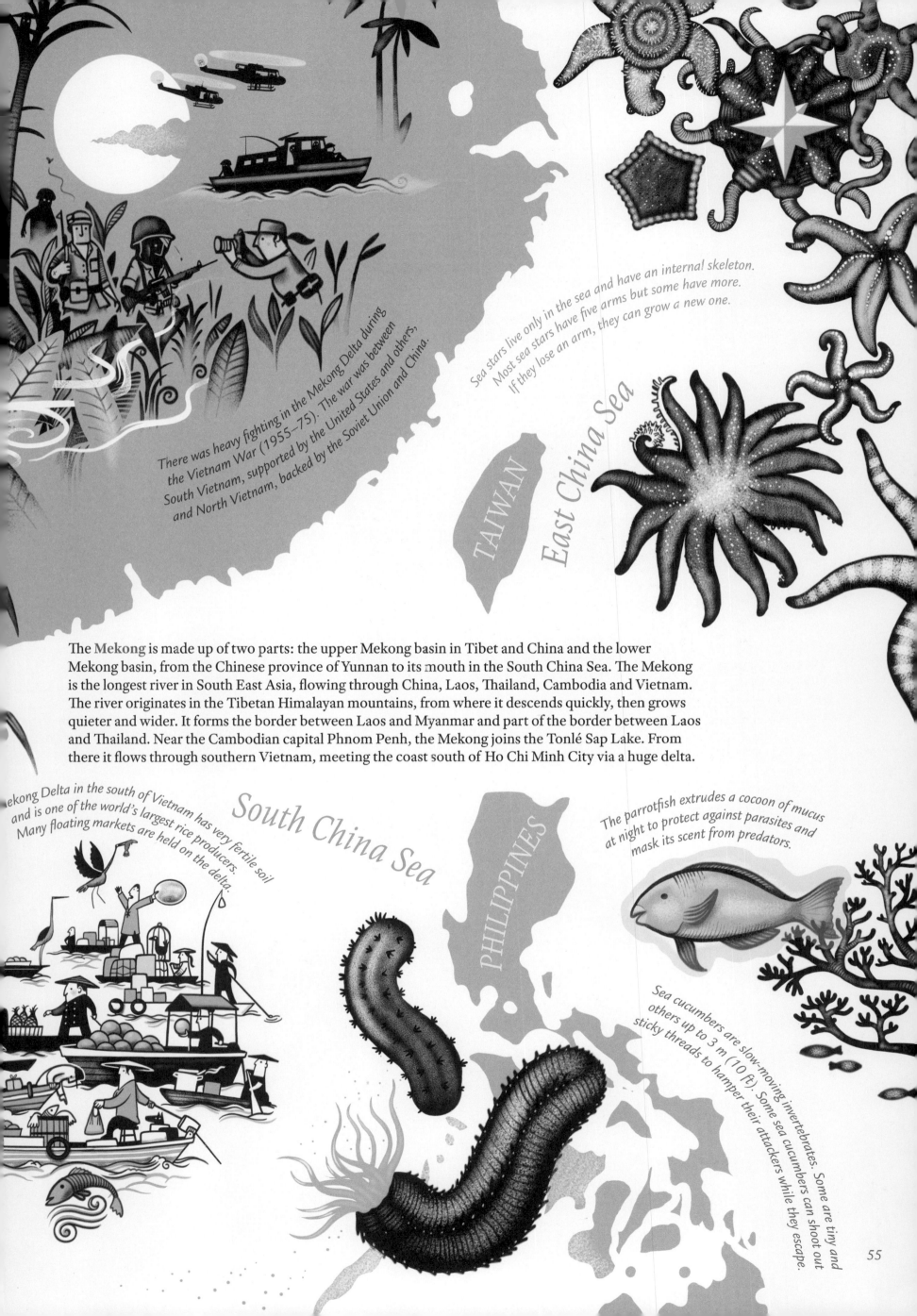

There was heavy fighting in the Mekong Delta during the Vietnam War (1955–75). The war was between South Vietnam, supported by the United States and others, and North Vietnam, backed by the Soviet Union and China.

Sea stars live only in the sea and have an internal skeleton. Most sea stars have five arms but some have more. If they lose an arm, they can grow a new one.

TAIWAN

East China Sea

The **Mekong** is made up of two parts: the upper Mekong basin in Tibet and China and the lower Mekong basin, from the Chinese province of Yunnan to its mouth in the South China Sea. The Mekong is the longest river in South East Asia, flowing through China, Laos, Thailand, Cambodia and Vietnam. The river originates in the Tibetan Himalayan mountains, from where it descends quickly, then grows quieter and wider. It forms the border between Laos and Myanmar and part of the border between Laos and Thailand. Near the Cambodian capital Phnom Penh, the Mekong joins the Tonlé Sap Lake. From there it flows through southern Vietnam, meeting the coast south of Ho Chi Minh City via a huge delta.

...ekong Delta in the south of Vietnam has very fertile soil and is one of the world's largest rice producers. Many floating markets are held on the delta.

South China Sea

PHILIPPINES

The parrotfish extrudes a cocoon of mucus at night to protect against parasites and mask its scent from predators.

Sea cucumbers are slow-moving invertebrates. Some are tiny and others up to 3 m (10 ft). Some sea cucumbers can shoot out sticky threads to hamper their attackers while they escape.

55

Whales and other cetaceans are large mammals even though they live in the water: they take in air through their lungs and give birth to live young. They have blowholes on top of their heads and when they surface they expel stale air and breathe in quickly. Whales are classified into two groups: baleen whales and toothed whales. Dolphins and porpoises are in fact toothed whales.

Baleen is a kind of sieve in the mouth that helps the whale filter fish, squid and plankton from the water.

Just like our fingerprint, the tail of every whale is unique. Each has its own patterns, scars and skin tone. This is how scientists can identify whales.

Plankton are small organisms that live just under the ocean's surface. Phytoplankton or vegetable plankton needs sunlight to make food. Zooplankton or animal plankton lives off the phytoplankton. Plankton forms the basis of the sea's food chain.

Senegal

Sierra Leone

Mo

South
Atlantic Ocean

White marlin

56

Mediterranean Sea

Tunisia

Algeria

The Sahara is the biggest desert on earth, covering more than 9 million km² (3½ million mi²).

Libya

Egypt

AFRICA

Niger

Mali

Niger

Chad

Nigeria

Sudan

Nile

Red Sea

It's easy to stay afloat in the Dead Sea because of its high concentration of salt.

Eritrea

Ethiopia

Central African Republic

South Sudan

Cameroon

Gulf of Guinea

Ghana

Benin

Togo

Gabon

Congo

Democratic Republic of Congo

Uganda

Rwanda

Burundi

Kenya

Somalia

Gulf of Aden

Tanzania

Anglerfish

... one knows for sure why flying fish "fly." ... might be that they glide briefly above ... water to escape from their enemies.

Angola

Zambia

Malawi

Mozambique

Mozambique Channel

Madagascar

Namibia

Zimbabwe

Botswana

South Africa

Cape of Good Hope

The coelacanth was rediscovered on the coast of South Africa in 1938. It was thought to have died out 66 million years ago.

Mediterranean Sea

Cairo, the city of a thousand minarets, is the capital of Egypt.

The Suez Canal links the Mediterranean Sea with the Red Sea, dividing Africa and Asia.

LIBYA

Alexandria

EGYPT

In the Bible story Moses parted the Red Sea with God's help so the Israelites could escape slavery in Egypt.

Giza is a suburb of Cairo famous for its ancient necropolis with large pyramids and the Sphinx.

The Aswan Dam was built to prevent the annual flooding of the Nile and to generate electricity.

Khartoum, the capital of Sudan, lies at the confluence of the Blue Nile and the White Nile.

Nile

Red Sea

In Egyptian mythology, the scarab, a dung beetle, is a sacred animal.

In ancient Egypt people believed that the god Hapi was responsible for annual flooding, which left rich silt on the banks of the Nile.

SUDAN

ERITREA

CHAD

For centuries nilometers were used to measure the water level of the Nile and to predict a good or bad harvest.

Blue Nile

CENTRAL AFRICAN REPUBLIC

SOUTH SUDAN

White Nile

Lake Tana in Ethiopia is the highest lake in Africa and the source of the Blue Nile. The lake contains several islands inhabited by cloistered monks. They guard the treasures of former Ethiopian emperors.

Adult hippopotamuses don't swim; they walk on the riverbed.

DEMOCRATIC REPUBLIC OF CONGO

Nile crocodile

ETHIOPIA

KENYA

Kilimanjaro is Africa's tallest mountain, consisting of three volcanoes: Kibo, Mawenzi and Shira.

UGANDA

Lake Victoria

RWANDA

BURUNDI

TANZANIA

Persian Gulf

Gulf of Oman

Gulf of Aden

The giant manta, with a span of up to 7 m (23 ft) and weighing as much as 1350 kg (3000 lb), is the largest ray in the world. It eats by filtering plankton and small fish.

Sharks and rays have a skeleton of pliable cartilage, not stiff bone. They have no swim bladder and will drown if they don't keep swimming.

Silky shark

Hammerhead shark

Sawfish

Oceanic whitetip

Bigeye thresher

Longfin mako

SOMALIA

Pirates remain a problem in Somalia. They board passing ships and demand ransom for the cargo and the crew.

Arabian Sea

The Nile is the world's longest river, flowing 6650 km (4100 mi) through northeast Africa. The Ancient Egyptian civilization developed on its banks, and farming originated on the fertile Nile Delta. The Nile begins in Burundi and Rwanda. From Lake Victoria it flows through Uganda, and through South Sudan and Sudan, where it is called the White Nile. It joins the Blue Nile in the city of Khartoum. Further northwards the Atbarah or Black Nile joins the main river. Both the Atbarah and the Blue Nile begin in the highlands of Ethiopia. The Nile continues to flow north through the deserts of Sudan and Egypt, then forms a delta north of Cairo, which empties into the Mediterranean Sea.

The Tuareg are nomadic Berber people who have lived in the Sahara for centuries. By tradition, the men veil their faces but the women do not.

The camel is known as the ship of the desert.

SENEGAL

A marsh on the Niger floods each year during the rainy season, making the ground very fertile. This inland delta is a vast breeding ground for birds and an important area for agriculture and fishing.

GUINEA

BURKINA FAS

The leopard's spots are called rosettes.

The source of the Niger lies in the highlands of Guinea, near the city of Tembakounda.

The West African manatee is found in coastal areas, rivers and lakes. Manatees, or sea cows, used to be mistaken for mermaids.

SIERRA LEONE

The **Niger** begins in Guinea and flows in a great loop into Mali. At its most northerly point, near the old city of Timbuktu, it runs alongside the Sahara. After that, the river bends southeast to Nigeria and continues southwards into the Gulf of Guinea to the west of Port Harcourt. The peculiar crescent curve of the river suggests that it was originally two rivers.

Gulf of Guinea

LIBERIA

IVORY COAST

Melon-headed dolphin

A European explorer asked an old man carrying a load of branches the name of the nearest town. The man didn't understand him, was scar and called out "min-chan m'bidjan" (I only took the leaves). That's reputedly how the port city of Abidjan got its name.

110 million years ago the Sarcosuchus imperator lived here, the largest crocodile ever. It was almost 12 m (40 ft) long and ate dinosaurs.

Niger

MALI

NIGER

Timbuktu was established as a trade hub in the 12th century. It also became a hub of Islamic learning. Its wealth and remoteness gave the city a mythical significance in the eyes of European Christians. The name Timbuktu is used by Europeans as a synonym for a distant place that's hard to reach.

An aardvark can eat 50,000 ants and termites in one night.

TOGO

BENIN

NIGERIA

Kainji Lake was formed by the construction of the Kainji Dam in 1968. A large national park surrounds the lake.

Anansi is a god descended to Earth who can take the form of a trickster spider. Anansi stories originated in present-day Ghana and spread throughout West Africa.

The city of Asaba is said to have been established by Nnebisi, a young man in search of his homeland. He carried a magic pot on his head, which would fall on the spot where he was born. The pot landed on the west bank of the Niger in southern Nigeria.

The Cameroon Line is a rift valley consisting of a stretch of volcanic mountains that extend into the sea, appearing there as islands.

The Gulf of Guinea holds a great supply of oil because of the huge volume of organic sediment the rivers have deposited in the sea over millions of years.

Every year there are hundreds of oil spills in the Niger Delta, with severe consequences for people and nature.

The Congo river consists of four parts. The first, the upper course, flows from the source river, Lualaba, to the city of Kisangani. The middle or second stretch starts here and goes to Kinshasa. In the third or lower course, from Kinshasa to Matadi, hydroelectric stations generate all of the electricity for the Democratic Republic of Congo. The final stretch is the ocean current, which flows under the seawater. The Congo is the world's deepest river and an important shipping link in Central Africa. However, seagoing ships cannot navigate the river because of the Livingstone Falls in the lower reaches.

CONGO

Congo

The Congo flows through the second-largest rainforest in the world.

There is a centuries-old legend about the Mokèlé-mbèmbé, "the that stops the river's flow." The huge creature that dwells in river bends appears in stories of the Pygmy people. The search for this beast has captured the imagination of adventurers from all over the world.

GABON

Kinshasa is the capital of the Democratic Republic of Congo. On the other side of the river lies Brazzaville, the capital of Congo.

DEMOCRATIC REPUBLIC OF CONGO

The Portuguese navigator Diogo Cão came upon the mouth of the Congo during his 15th-century exploration when he noticed that the seawater was becoming fresher.

Matadi and Boma are two important port towns on the Congo. The Livingstone Falls and rapids further up make a long section of the Congo unnavigable. A railway bypasses the 38 waterfalls between Matadi and Kinshasa.

ANGOLA

The Democratic Republic of Congo became independent in 1960, having been claimed by Belgium as the private property of King Leopold II and then as a Belgian colony. Patrice Lumumba was briefly its first prime minister, then Joseph Kasavubu the first president.

Kisangani

Mountain gorillas, the largest gorillas, are seriously threatened. They live in the Virunga Mountains in the Democratic Republic of Congo, Uganda and Rwanda.

UGANDA

Lake Victoria

Congolese rumba, a combination of rumba and jazz, began in the 1940s and spread in various forms to European dance clubs.

Lualaba

RWANDA

BURUNDI

Under the government of the Belgian king, Leopold II, people were forced to work in horrific conditions in what was then the Congo Free State.

Lake Tanganyika

TANZANIA

Okapi

Luvua

The Democratic Republic of Congo has more than 200 languages. Since its period under Belgian rule, the official language is French and there are four national languages: Lingala, Kikongo, Swahili and Tshiluba.

Lake Mweru

Henry Morton Stanley was a journalist and explorer. In 1869 he was sent to look for the vanished explorer David Livingstone. Seeing a white man at Lake Tanganyika, he spoke the famous words: "Dr. Livingstone, I presume?"

By eating a lot of fruit and nuts and scattering undamaged seeds in its dung, the African bush elephant spreads the greatest number of trees and bushes of all the world's animals.

ZAMBIA

A crocodile cries while it eats to clean its eyes, not because it's upset. Crying crocodile tears is a phrase used to describe someone who pretends to be sad.

The saltwater crocodile is the largest reptile in the world.

The Pacific Ocean is the world's largest and deepest ocean. The _____ the Philippine Sea is the deepest underwater place yet known. A two-pers__ sea submersible reached the bottom in 1960. Scientists had thought nothing could survive the water pressure but found small fish living there.

South China Sea

Philippine Sea

Andaman Sea

Gulf of Thailand

Malaysia

Indonesia

Java Sea

Banda Sea

Papua New Guinea

Fly

Bismarck Sea

Solomo_

Indian Ocean

Timor Sea

Arafura Sea

Cora_

Many Aboriginal peoples share a belief in the Dreaming, the time when ancestral beings shaped the world, creating land, sea, animals, plants and peoples. One of these beings is the Rainbow Serpent.

Australia

Great Australian Bight

Darling

Murray

Bass Strait

The sea monsters and snakes on early sea charts might be based on the oarfish, which can grow to 11 m (36 ft).

The mission of the British Challenger Expedition of 1872–76 was to explore the oceans. HMS Challenger, a warship, was transformed into an exploratory vessel, and its scientists collected material that took them 20 years to examine. Their published work laid the foundation for present-day oceanography.

Octopuses are intelligent invertebrate animals that can squeeze themselves through the smallest openings and can even live out of water, solve puzzles, squirt ink and change the pigment and pattern of their skin.

Molluscs are "living fossils," having changed very little for hundreds of millions of years. They live in the front chamber of their shell; the other chambers are filled with gas and liquids that the animal uses to regulate its rising or sinking in the water.

Some stories from Polynesia tell of a spirit-ship that carries away the soul of a drowned person.

Pacific Ocean

Most sperm whales live in groups. They feed mainly on squid, including the giant squid. In the book Moby-Dick by the American writer Herman Melville, Captain Ahab obsessively hunted a great white sperm whale, which had bitten off his leg.

Tasman Sea

Waikato

New Zealand

A colossal squid was caught in the Ross Sea in 2007. The colossal squid is the largest squid species—bigger than the giant squid—and is believed to be an aggressive predator, with hooks as well as suckers on its arms.

People have lived in New Guinea for at least 40,000 years. There are more than 1000 indigenous groups, most with their own language, an estimated 44 of whom have no contact with the Western world.

Bananas have been cultivated in Papua New Guinea for 6500 years.

Fly

INDONESIA

PAPUA NEW GUINEA

Wild pig

The Italian naturalist and explorer Luigi D'Albertis undertook violent forays up the Fly River in the name of exploration in the late 19th century. His methods were criticized by contemporary explorers and administrators alike.

The Fly is a meandering river. When water makes a turn, the water on the outside flows faster, eroding the outer bank and depositing sediment on the slower-flowing inside of the turn. Over time, meanders are formed with ever-widening bends. The bends are named after the Turkish river Meander.

Archerfish live in South East Asi They squirt their prey with a jet of water.

...w's tree kangaroo can jump ...n from 10 m (33 ft) high in a tree without hurting itself.

The New Guinea quoll can bear up to 30 young at a time but raises only six from each litter—that being the number of teats in her pouch.

Papuan hornbill

A sugar glider in flight.

The Fly river is the longest undammed river in the world and, partly because of the huge annual rainfall, has the largest flow of any in Oceania. The Fly begins in the Star Mountains in Papua New Guinea. The upper reaches of the river flow through almost impenetrable rainforest. The Fly empties through a delta into the Gulf of Papua and the Coral Sea, in a wide, mangrove-covered estuary. When the first Europeans visited in 1845, the British naval officer Francis Blackwood named the river after his ship, the *Fly*.

Sea turtles mate at sea. The females later lay their eggs in deep holes on the beach. When the eggs hatch, the small turtles dash to the water: a short but dangerous journey.

Global warming is putting the survival of sea turtles at risk.

Coral consists of very small creatures, which live mostly in colonies. Soft corals are flexible and often look like plants. Stony corals have a hard skeleton made from limestone, and they form beds and reefs. Great Barrier Reef in the Coral Sea along the coast of Australia is the world's largest coral reef system.

Gulf of Papua

Lake Torrens is one of the largest salt lakes in Australia. It is a closed basin with no outlet to the sea. It loses water only through evaporation.

Lake Torrens is one of more than 12,000 Important Bird and Biodiversity Areas of the world—significant places for bird conservation

Stories of the bunyip have taug generations of Australian children to respect the rivers and waterways.

A koala gets moisture from eucalyptus leaves. It hardly ever drinks.

The Darling has been badly affected by water pollution and extreme drought, and many of its native fish are now rare or extinct.

The platypus is an egg-laying mamma The male has a poisonous spur on its hind legs.

Lake Torrens

Spencer Gulf

Gulf St Vincent

Kangaroo Island

Darling

AUSTRALIA

Murray

Melbourne is the largest seaport i Australia.

The area where Melbourne now lies has been the home of the Kulin nation for over 40,000 years.

In 1626 François Thijssen was commissioned by the Dutch East India Company to chart the coast of Terra Australis.

Barracudas

Boomerang

The male malleefowl builds a large nest mound with leaves, sticks and bark where the female lays her eggs. The chicks must scratch their way to the surface of the mound after they break out of their eggs.

When a miner found gold in 1851, many people came to Australia to join the gold rush.

New South Wales was established in 1788 as a penal colony for English convicts.

Didgeridoo

Many Aboriginal peoples pass on stories from the Dreaming from generation to generation.

Sydney is the oldest and largest city in Australia.

Canberra is the capital of Australia.

Murrumbidgee

Charles Sturt was the first European to explore the Murrumbidgee and Murray rivers in the 1830s.

Mount Kosciuszko in the Snowy Mountains is the highest mountain on the Australian continent. It is part of the Australian Alps and the Great Dividing Range.

Tasman Sea

Arnoux's beaked whale is one of the largest dolphins in the world. It hunts squid and cuttlefish.

The Murray, Australia's longest river, is the principal river of the Murray–Darling Basin. It begins in the Snowy Mountains, the highest part of the Australian Alps, and flows through the Australian interior to the Pacific Ocean.

The Darling originates in the Great Dividing Range, not far from the east coast near the border between New South Wales and Queensland. The river flows through New South Wales and joins the Murray at Wentworth. The Murray–Darling Basin is one of the largest in the world with a surface area of about 1 million km² (385,000 mi²).

Bass Strait

Hauraki Gulf

Firth of Thames

Auckland's Sky Tower is the tallest free-standing structure in the southern hemisphere.

The Waikato and Waipā rivers come together at Ngāruawāhia, an important port for commerce in the 19th century.

Two Australian schoolfriends and adventurers, Cas and Jonesy, crossed the Tasman Sea in a kayak in 2008.

In 1904, school principal Mary Isabel Fraser brought seeds of the Chinese gooseberry back from China. In the 1930s, Hayward Wright used them to develop the green kiwifruit we know today.

Polynesian stick charts were among the earliest nautical maps. The bamboo sticks and shells indicated sea routes, currents and islands.

Hamilton or Kirikiriroa, which means long strip of gravel, is the largest inland city in New Zealand.

Hobbiton film set

Tasman Sea

In 1642, Dutch explorer Abel Tasman was the first European to reach New Zealand.

Waikato

The Treaty of Waitangi is New Zealand's founding document, designed as a partnership between Māori and the British Crown. The English and Māori versions of the Treaty had different meanings, especially about sovereignty and land ownership. Friction over its interpretation led to a series of wars during the mid-19th century.

Huka Falls

Lake Taupō

Rainbow trout

70

The North Island's **Waikato** is New Zealand's longest river. The river has its source on the slopes of Mount Ruapehu in Tongariro National Park, where it joins the Tongariro River. It continues through Lake Taupō and runs via the Huka Falls to the northwest, finally meeting the Tasman Sea. The Waikato is spiritually and physically significant for the Māori who have lived on its banks, particularly the Tainui and Ngāti Tūwharetoa tribes.

White Island or Whakaari is an active offshore volcano.

Polynesian voyagers navigated and discovered a large part of the South Pacific over thousands of years. They knew where they were based on the position of the sun, stars, currents, waves, the migratory patterns of birds, the temperature of the water, stick charts and stories passed down. These methods are still taught today as survival advice for anyone shipwrecked.

The taniwha lives in deep water or dark caves and is a powerful spiritual being in Māori mythology. It can assume different shapes, such as a great shark or gigantic lizard.

Bay of Plenty

The haka is a ceremonial Māori dance.

The little blue penguin expels the excess salt it absorbs from seawater through salt glands in its nostrils.

NEW ZEALAND

New Zealanders are often called Kiwis, a name drawn from the kiwi, a flightless native bird. The male mating call sounds like "kiwi."

The short-finned mako is the fastest shark in the world and can leap high out of the water.

Hawke Bay

The early decades of the 20th century are known as the "heroic era" of Antarctic exploration, as European explorers raced to be the first to reach the pole and cross the Antarctic continent.

Leopard seals prefer to live alone, coming together only to mate.

South polar skua

Weddell Sea

A great deal of the Weddell Sea is made up of ice.

Patagonian toothfish

Filchner-Ronne Ice Shelf

Bellingshausen Sea

Crocodile icefish have adapted well to icy water. Their metabolism is slower, and they have special blood vessels and a larger heart.

The snow petrel breeds only in Antarctica. It protects its nest by spitting smelly oil at aggressors.

No one owns Antarctica. In the Antarctic Treaty of 1961 different countries agreed that the south polar region would be used only for peaceful and scientific purposes.

Amundsen Sea

Southern Ocean

or Antarctic Ocean

A research vessel and icebreaker belonging to the US Coast Guard.